TRY NOT TO LAUGH CHALLENGE

LAUGH CHALLENGE

Joke Book

LOL

For Girls!

Edition

HOWLING MOON BOOKS

HOWLING
MOON BOOKS

Try Not to Laugh Challenge!

Rules:

Pick your team, or go one on one.

Sit across from each other & make eye contact.

Take turns reading jokes to each other.

You can make silly faces, funny sound effects, etc.

When your opponent laughs or cracks a smile, you get a point!

First team to win 3 points, **Wins!**

Telling Jokes Builds Confident Kids, & Laughter Makes Everyone Happy!

How do you add glitter to
s'mores?

Use GLAM-crackers!

What kind of music do you listen
to when you go for a hike?

A trail mix!

What do you say to kittens
who are late getting ready
for school?

FURRY up!

What's another name for invisible ink?

INK-cognito!

Who is number 2 on Santa's list?

The poop emoji!

What food is the most curious?

Wonder bread!

What does Elsa's ringtone sound like?

Brrr-ring!

How do dogs start a race?

On your BARK, get set, go!

Who takes your cell phone if you leave it under your pillow?

The BLUE-TOOTH fairy!

Why did the laptop go to the
eye doctor?

To improve its WEB-sight!

What do you call a singing
contest for ghosts?

SCARE-eoke!

Why did the family visit
Mount Rushmore?

Because it is HEADS above
the other monuments!

What kind of email does a garbage man get?

JUNK mail!

Why did Cinderella's shoe fart?

Because it was a GAS slipper!

Why are swimmers good at soccer?

Because they are good at DIVING for the ball!

Where does the girl detective go undercover?

In her bed!

What did the sleepy cat say to the mouse?

CATCH you later!

Why couldn't the little mermaid find a bathing suit top at the store?

Because she was shopping in Bikini Bottom!

Why did the family enjoy
watching the fireworks?

Because they got a BANG
out of it!

What is a hiker's favorite drink?

Mountain Dew!

What do you say to a nervous
pair of new cleats?

Get a GRIP!

What is a math teacher's
favorite video game?

Disney Infinity!

Knock knock.
Who's there?
Lego.
Lego who?

Lego of the past!

What kind of word game
is angry?

Mad-Libs!

Why didn't the horse trainer want the promotion?

She didn't want to be SADDLED with a lot more work!

Why won't Ariel go into the kitchen?

She is afraid of the cabi-NETS!

Why did the unicorn go to the horseshoe store?

To get her KICKS!

How did the alien bookworms
find Belle?

They said, "Take me to your
READER!"

Why did the tablespoon break
up with the teaspoon?

It didn't measure up!

Who is good at finding errors
in new books?

Miss Print!

How do singers talk to each other?

With musical NOTES!

What does a drama queen say before she makes a video?

"Lights. Camera. Reaction!"

Why was the cell phone mad?

People kept pushing his buttons!

Where do unicorns shop?

Old NEIGH-vy!

What is the coolest sandwich?

An ice cream sandwich!

What is the most expensive cookie?

A fortune cookie!

How do singers talk to each
other?

With musical NOTES!

What does a drama queen say
before she makes a video?

"Lights. Camera. Reaction!"

Why was the cell phone mad?

People kept pushing his buttons!

Where do unicorns shop?

Old NEIGH-vy!

What is the coolest sandwich?

An ice cream sandwich!

What is the most expensive cookie?

A fortune cookie!

What is a llama's favorite drink?

Llama-nade!

What do genies wash their hair with?

LAMP-poo!

Why do social media stars have good eyesight?

Because they get millions of views!

What is the Pope's favorite scent?

POPE-pourri!

What kind of party do you throw
to find out which one of your
friends is the biggest shopper?

A SPENDER Reveal Party!

Which soccer player takes the
goal home after every game?

The goalkeeper!

What is a soda's favorite subject?

FIZZ-ics!

What is Elsa's favorite grocery store?

Trader SNOWS!

Where did The Three Bears go to fix little bear's broken chair?

Build-A-CHAIR Workshop!

What kind of candy should you eat before taking a test?

Smarties!

What was the dog doing on the soccer field?

He was the RUFF-eree!

Why do field hockey players make good friends?

Because they like to STICK together!

Why should you be extra nice to cats?

Because it is so easy to hurt their FELINES!

When should you buy a bird?

When it is going CHEAP!

Knock knock.
Who's there?
Handsome.
Handsome who?

Handsome of that popcorn
to me, please!

Knock knock.
Who's there?
Dozen.
Dozen who?

Dozen anyone want to build
a snowman?

Knock knock.
Who's there?
Herd.
Herd who?

Herd you were having a
dance party, so here I am!

Knock knock.
Who's there?
Cher.
Cher who?

Cher would be fun to
do a makeover!

Knock knock.
Who's there?
Wayne.
Wayne who?

Wayne are we going to
eat those doughnuts?

Knock knock.
Who's there?
Needle.
Needle who?

I needle to buy a mermaid
sleeping bag!

Who is the poop emoji's hero?

Super Pooper!

What princess is the life of
the party?

Rapunzel, she knows how
to let her hair down!

How do dogs surf the internet?

On their LAB-top computers!

What is the worse name you can give a zebra?

SPOT!

Why don't socks ever get married?

Because they don't stay together long enough!

Why doesn't Elsa worry about eating her ice cream too fast?

Because a brain freeze is SNOW big deal!

What is a vampire's favorite sport?

BAT-mitton!

Why do girls like to twirl when they are trying on dresses?

Because it is fun to take their dress for spin!

Why did the lollipop take karate lessons?

Because it was tired of being LICKED!

Why were the kids afraid of the milk?

Because it turned BAD!

Did you hear about the paper doll who farted?

She accidentally let one RIP!

Where does a dog keep his bone?

In the RUFF-frigerator!

Why couldn't Mrs. Potato Head answer her phone?

She was still putting her face on!

Why did the rabbit jump over the moon?

To look for the cow!

What position does a ghost play in soccer?

Dead Center!

Knock knock.
Who's there?
Wanda.
Wanda who?

Wanda have a karaoke contest?

Knock knock.
Who's there?
Bette.
Bette who?

Bette you can't guess what
my new favorite song is!

What philosopher pondered ways
to keep his feet warm?

SOCK-rates!

Why was the girl scout so good
at setting up the tents?

Because she knows the ROPES!

Why can't Sleeping Beauty make
a quick decision?

She always needs to SLEEP on it!

Why aren't pig jokes funny?

Because they're so BOAR-ing!

What do you call a teacher in charge of detention?

Miss Behave!

Why are cats helpful in the kitchen?

Because they always bring their WHISK-ers!

Why are computer jobs so time consuming for bunnies?

Because they go down too many rabbit holes!

Why were the kids getting tired during color time?

They were using cra-YAWNS!

Why don't bananas get lonely?

Because they hang around in bunches!

How is a dancer like a fitbit?

They are both full of steps!

Why did the dad try to cook a
hamburger on the grill
of his car?

He was at a CAR-beque!

What do teachers put on their
lasagne?

GRADED cheese!

What kind of things do sheep
like to paint?

LAMB-scapes!

How do you make gluten-free
pizza crust?

With cauli-FLOUR!

Where do bankers like to shop?

J.C. Penny's!

What happens when all the
princesses decide to have their
wedding on the same day?

You have a MARRY-thon!

Why doesn't Shrek think jokes are funny?

Because they go OGRE his head!

What kind of fruit does Donkey like?

DRAGON Fruit!

What is Fiona's favorite boy band?

Five SHREK-onds of Summer!

How do unicorns text?

Horse Code!

Why doesn't Elsa go to school?

Because every day is a
SNOW day!

How do witches call one another?

On their SPELL phones!

Why is Pegasus a good teacher?

Because he takes his students
under his wing!

What do teachers at Hogwarts use to grade their tests?

A magic marker!

Why do basketball players need
their passports with them
at all times?

In case they are caught
traveling!

What kind of school teaches
potty training?

PEE-school!

Why was the firefly getting
bigger?

He was GLOWING up!

Who is the mermaid afraid of?

The COD-father!

What did the unicorn want for her birthday?

An apple gift card!

What is the narwhal's favorite restaurant?

Red Lobster!

Why couldn't the sneaker afford to go out to lunch?

Because he was on a shoestring budget!

Why did the boy feel better after he took his shirt off?

Because he needed to get something off his chest!

What do squirrels put on their sandwiches?

NUT-ella!

Where do angels get married?

On Cloud Nine!

Why did the girl buy a selfie stick?

She needed some distance from taking too many selfies!

Why didn't the girl want to be friends with the dragon?

Because she didn't want to play with fire!

When is the best time to buy windows?

A CLEAR-ance Sale!

Why is a planetarium a bad place to study astronomy?

Because everyone SPACES out there!

What kind of food do tornado chasers eat?

Funnel cakes!

What do cows wear in Hawaii?

A MOO-MOO!
(Muumuu)

Why did the girl quit her violin lessons?

They were a pain in the NECK!

What kind of pen has mood swings?

A PEN-dulum!

Why is a sad movie like chopping onions?

Both are real TEAR-jerkers!

Why don't you want to play truth or dare games with dogs?

Because they will double-dog dare you!

Why do clams live in the mud,
below the saltwater?

They are hiding from the people
who want to PRY into
their lives!

What is the coolest invention?

Air conditioning!

Who knows how to fight crime
without batting an eye?

Batgirl!

What do you call a grumpy cow?

MOO-dy!

Why were the girls hopping mad?

Because they weren't allowed in the BOUNCE house!

Why does everyone like pizza night?

No matter how you SLICE it, it is the best night of the week!

What is the Poop Emoji's favorite scent?

POOP-pourri!

How do trees move around?

On hover-boards!

What do you say to a chatty marker?

Put a LID on it!

Why did the girl adopt a dog?

She wanted to get a new leash on life!

What do you call a sad stick?

A BUMMER-ang!

Why is it fun to get a bullseye?

Because you know that you
are right on TARGET!

What sport gets straight to
the point?

Fencing, because all other
sports are pointless!

What do pimples do while you sleep?

Nothing, they just ZIT there!

Why wasn't Cinderella good at dribbling the soccer ball?

Because she kept running away from it!

What happens when trees try to make maple syrup?

It is a STICKY situation!

Where does Santa shop for bad boys and girls?

Coal's
(Kohl's)

Why did the famous cat sit on top of the Christmas tree?

Because she thinks she's a star!

What do Santa's elves post on Social Media?

Elf-ies!

Why are mermaids so calm?

They just float through life!

Why are llamas so happy?

Because they have no prob-llamas!

Why do pirates always wear hats?

Because they have too many
bad hair days!

Why did the volleyball website crash?

Because they were having trouble
with their SERVER!

Why doesn't fire have any friends?

It always burns its bridges!

What did one candle say to
the other?

Don't birthdays just BURN
you up!

How do you get the sun to rise
early?

Dance the night away!

Why do kids always look busy on the school bus?

It is their last chance to finish their homework!

How much honey do honey badgers eat?

None of your beeswax!

Why did the girl want to be a chef?

It is a tasteful profession!

Why are unicorns so healthy?

An apple a day keeps the
doctor away!

**What do superheroes like to put
in their drinks?**

Just ice!

**Why did the dog want to be
a cheerleader?**

Because she was a
POM-POMeranian!

What do you do if life gets boring?

Get glasses, it will change the
way you LOOK at things!

What kind of road can't you drive
on?

A railroad!

How do you know if koalas are in charge of the school cafeteria?

The KOALITY of your food goes way up!

What is a banana's favorite
gymnastic move?

The split!

What plant likes ghosts?

Bam-BOO!

Where can you learn "baby talk"?

Mommy bloggers!

What is Pegasus' motto?

If at first you don't succeed,
FLY, FLY again!

Where is the happiest place to be at a carnival?

The Merry-Go-Round!

Why was the blogger cold?

She was always surrounded
by DRAFTS!

**What pens are easiest to get
along with?**

Gel pens!

**What has a burning desire to
light up the sky?**

Fireworks!

What kind of mexican food do cats like?

PURR-ittos!

What instrument does Rapunzel play?

A HAIR-monica!

What happened when the girl received a flood of emails?

She got CARRIED AWAY reading them!

How was One Direction rated when they first started touring?

Five Stars!

What kind of music do you listen to if you have braces?

Heavy Metal!

Why did the cell phone go to the dentist?

It had a BLUE-TOOTH!

What is a good verse to sing from "Call Me Maybe" after telling someone a joke?

Here's my joke
And this is crazy
I know it's funny
So laugh at it maybe!

What infects the internet?

VIRAL videos!

Where do most superheroes live?

CAPE Town!

Why was the girl trying to save 1,000 dollars?

She wanted to buy a GRAND piano!

How do ghouls workout to music?

TOMB-ba!
(Zomba)

What is a cow's favorite restaurant?

Chick-fil-A!

When is a selfie not a selfie?

When it has been PHOTO BOMBED!

Where do rainbows keep their computer files?

In the CLOUD!

What kind of test should you never give to a pimple?

A POP quiz!

What kind of games do hash browns play?

Hash-tag!
(#)

Who has the worst multiple personality identity disorder?

Emoticons!

What kind of food does Ariel like?

Seaweed snacks!

Where does Peter Pan shop for clothes?

Never 21!

What are the coolest things to write?

FAN fictions!

Where do boy bands stay when they are touring?

At the INN-Sync!

What kind of pen does a pirate use?

A paper-mateyyy!

What kind of vehicle does Frankenstein drive?

A MONSTER truck!

What kind of soup do vampires eat?

Alpha-BAT soup!

Why did the chef cross the road?

To get to the FOOD truck!

What is a volleyball player's favorite dog?

A SETTER!

Why did the boy bury the video game controller?

The batteries were dead!

What kind of cowboy farts the most?

A rootin' tootin' cowboy!

Who is the most patriotic woman?

Lady Liberty!

Why are skeletons patriotic?

Because they are BONE
in the USA!

Why are monsters cool?

Because they are Creepin'
it real!

Why are smoothies popular?

Because they know how to
BLEND in!

What is a cell phone's motto?

Always be your selfie!

What is a spider's favorite kind of rice?

Sticky rice!

What kind of fruit do astronauts like to eat?

STAR fruit!

What instrument does a cucumber play?

A PICKLE-lo!

What happened to One Direction?

They all went their SEPARATE ways!

Why don't skunks like shopping malls?

Because they like to
ODOR online!

Why don't envelopes and letter sets move?

Because they're STATIONARY!

What is a geologist's favorite music?

Hard Rock!

What is a pen's favorite color?

P-INK!

What kind of pillows like to fight?

THROW pillows!

What did Snow White say after
her pictures got stuck in
the photo booth?

Some day my PRINTS will come!

What is a cheerleader's favorite drink?

ROOT Beer!

Why does the soccer ball like to show off?

Because it gets a KICK out of it!

Why do golfer's prefer a salad over a grinder for lunch?

They try to stay away from sand wedges! (sandwiches)

How many hours will your first
golf game take to play?

It could take FORE ever!

Why wasn't Cinderella a good
soccer player?

Because she had a pumpkin for
a coach!

Sparkle highlighters are the pens
of the future...

MARK my words!

Why should you always have
balloons at a slumber party?

Because they are good at
staying UP all night!

What does a waitress and
volleyball player have in common?

They are both good SERVERS!

Why did the tennis player only
want nine lessons?

Because TENNIS too many!

Why did the cheerleader only want to practice pyramids on Saturday?

Because Monday through Friday are WEAK days!

What did Cinderella wear at swim practice?

Glass FLIPPERS!

How do you know when you are playing better in golf?

A BIRDIE will tell you!

Why did the hot dog study so hard?

He wanted to be on the honor ROLL!

How do you keep other people out of your bedroom?

Make sure your floor is full of Legos!

What is a ghoul's favorite game?

Hide and GHOST Seek!

Why was the rock in the dance routine?

Because it was a STEPPING stone!

What is Elsa's favorite game?

Tic-Tac-SNOW!

Why did the girl stand on her desk in drama class?

Because the teacher told her to take it from the TOP!

What is a dinosaur's favorite song?

I Love You, You Love Me...!

Why can't popular boy bands play follow the leader?

Because they have too many followers!

What should you do if an
orthodontist wants
to tell you a joke?

BRACE yourself!

What is a dog's favorite food?

A PUPITO!

How long does it take a horse
to lose a race?

Only a 2nd!

What kind of phone should
Tinkerbell use?

A micro-phone!

What do you call a black and
white pen?

A PEN-guin!

Why didn't the girl throw away
all of her old socks?

Because she got cold feet!

What do you call zombies who
never went to school?

The unread!

What do you give computer
teachers at the end of
the school year?

GIF baskets!

What kind of humor does an
old gel pen have?

Dry!

Why did the bee enter the
singing contest?

She thought it was a STINGING
contest!

Why aren't pigs allowed in
photo booths?

Because they HOG it!

What makes music on your head?

A head-BAND!

What dinosaur wanted to take voice lessons?

Tyranno-CHORUS rex!

What do you call a girl who wears different color socks?

Miss Match!

What happens if life gets a little crazy?

Get braces, it will straighten things out!

Knock knock.
Who's there?
Icy.
Icy who?

Icy you shopping on your phone!

Knock knock.
Who's there?
Wooden.
Wooden who?

Wooden you like to know
what my password is!

Knock knock.
Who's there?
Gopher.
Gopher who?

I could gopher an ice cream
cone right now!

Knock knock.
Who's there?
Mint.
Mint who?

I mint to tell you that I'm
wearing my unicorn onesie
to school tomorrow!

Knock knock.
Who's there?
Will.
Will who?

When the cats away, the
mice Will play!

Knock knock.
Who's there?
Sick.
Sick who?

I was sick as a dog yesterday!

Knock knock.
Who's there?
Doughnut.
Doughnut who?

Doughnut be afraid to
follow your dreams!

Knock knock.
Who's there?
Lettuce.
Lettuce who?

Lettuce know when the
coast is clear!

Knock knock.
Who's there?
Time.
Time who?

Time flies when you are
having fun!

Knock knock.
Who's there?
Owl.
Owl who?

That's Owl Folks!

Thanks for helping us spread
some fun and laughter with the
Try Not to Laugh Challenge
Girls Edition Joke Book!

Please consider leaving us a review
on Amazon.com. We value your
feedback & greatly appreciate
your time!

Thank you

Howling Moon Books

Available from Howling Moon Books

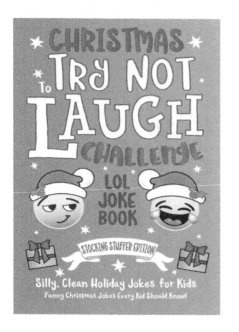

Available from Howling Moon Books

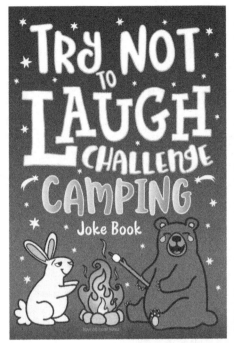

Available from Howling Moon Books

Available from Howling Moon Books

Made in the USA
Middletown, DE
08 December 2019